# MAKE YOUR OWN SUGAR SKULLS CUT-OUT & COLOR PARTY BOOK

## MASKS - WALL DECORATIONS - BUNTING
### ILLUSTRATED BY ANTONY BRIGGS

THIS BOOK BELONGS TO

..............................

ALL IMAGES COPYRIGHT ANTONY BRIGGS 2016

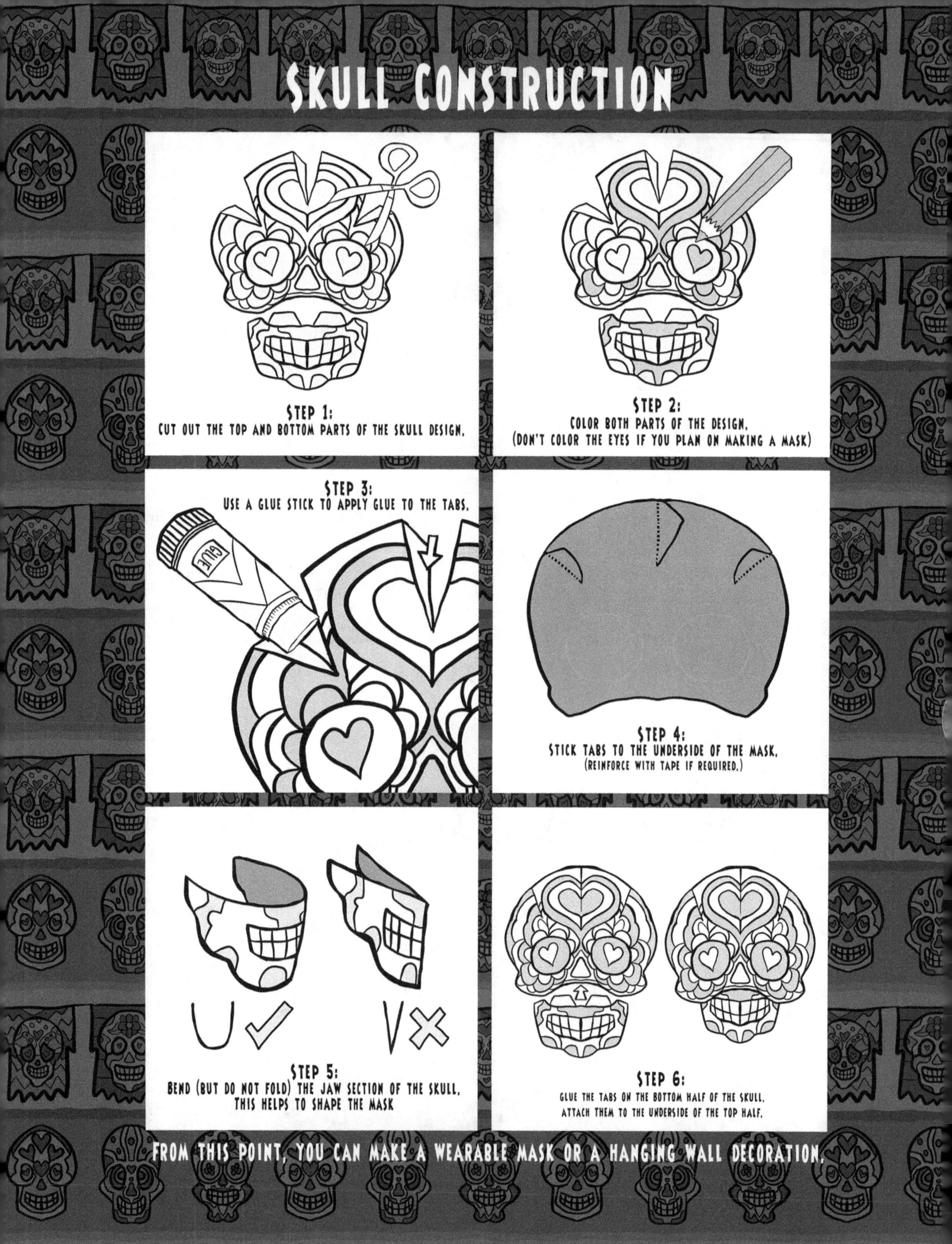

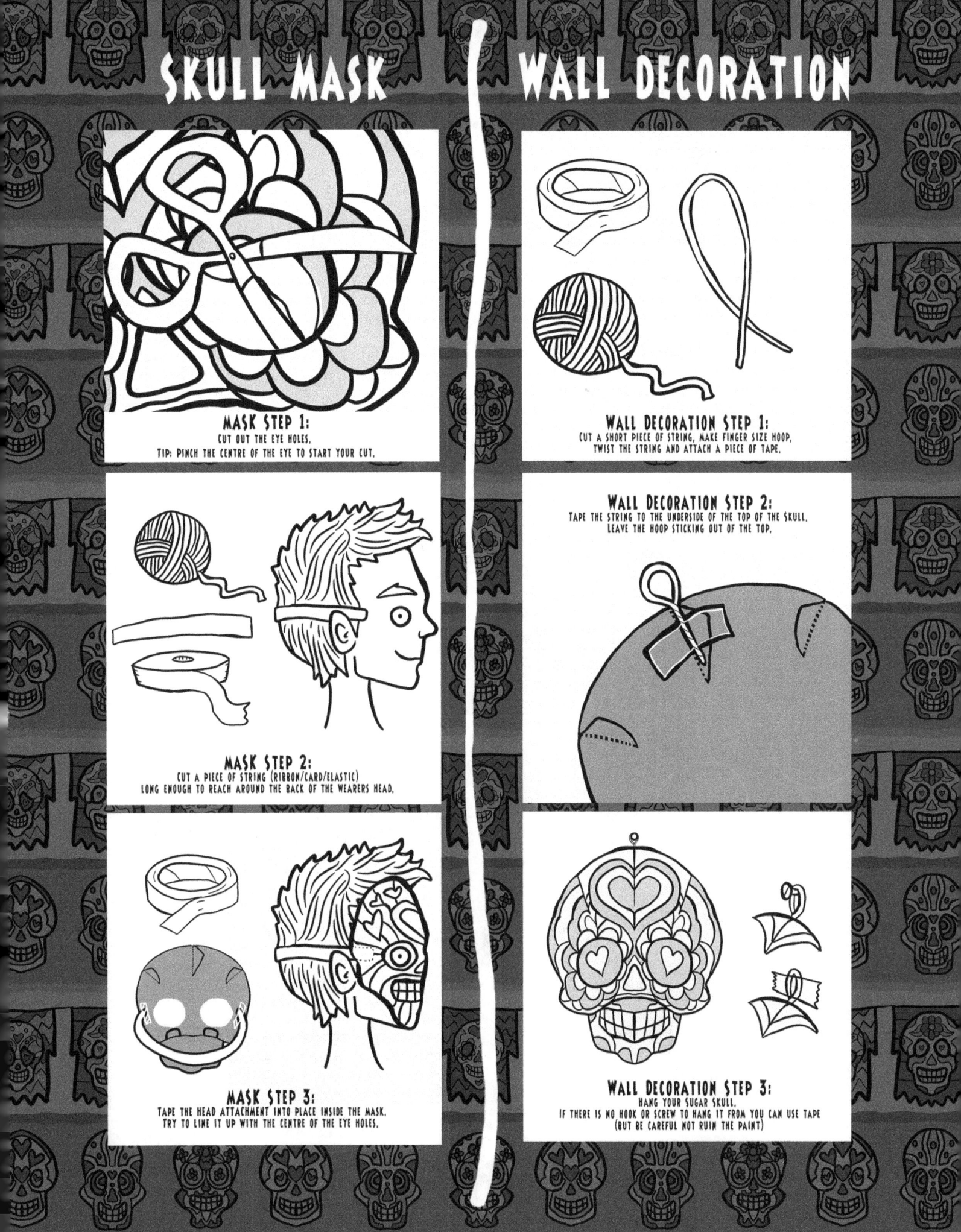

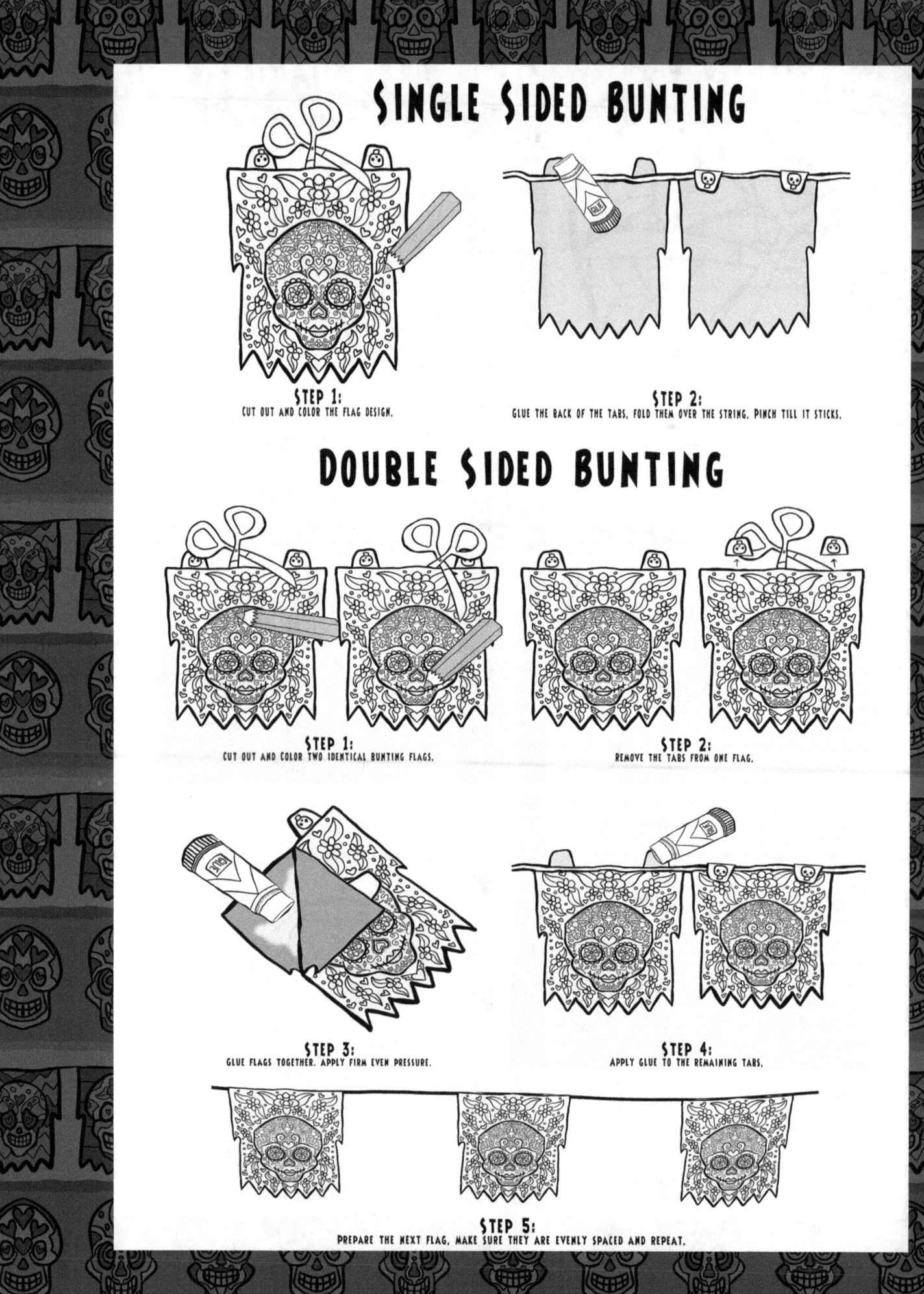

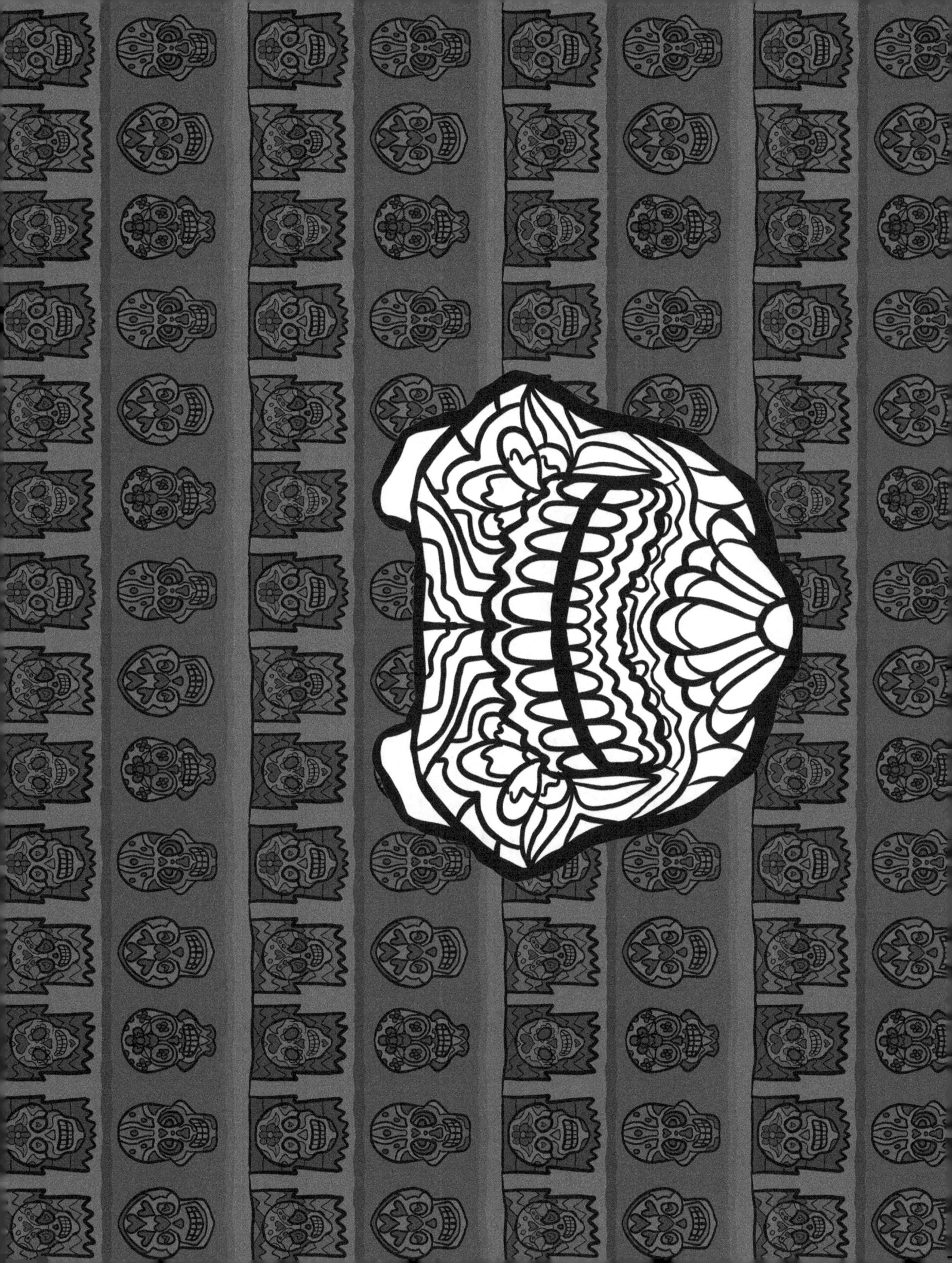

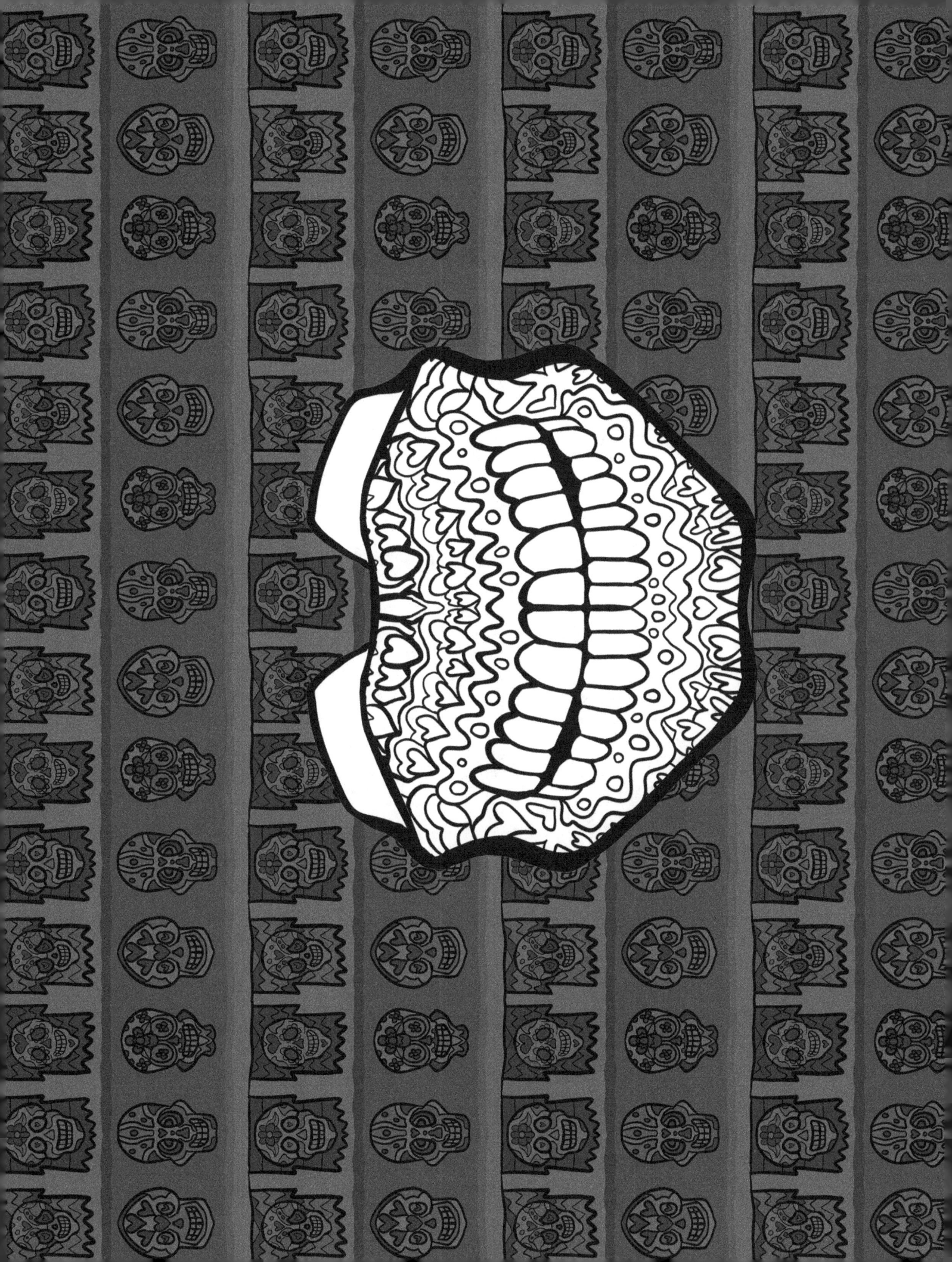

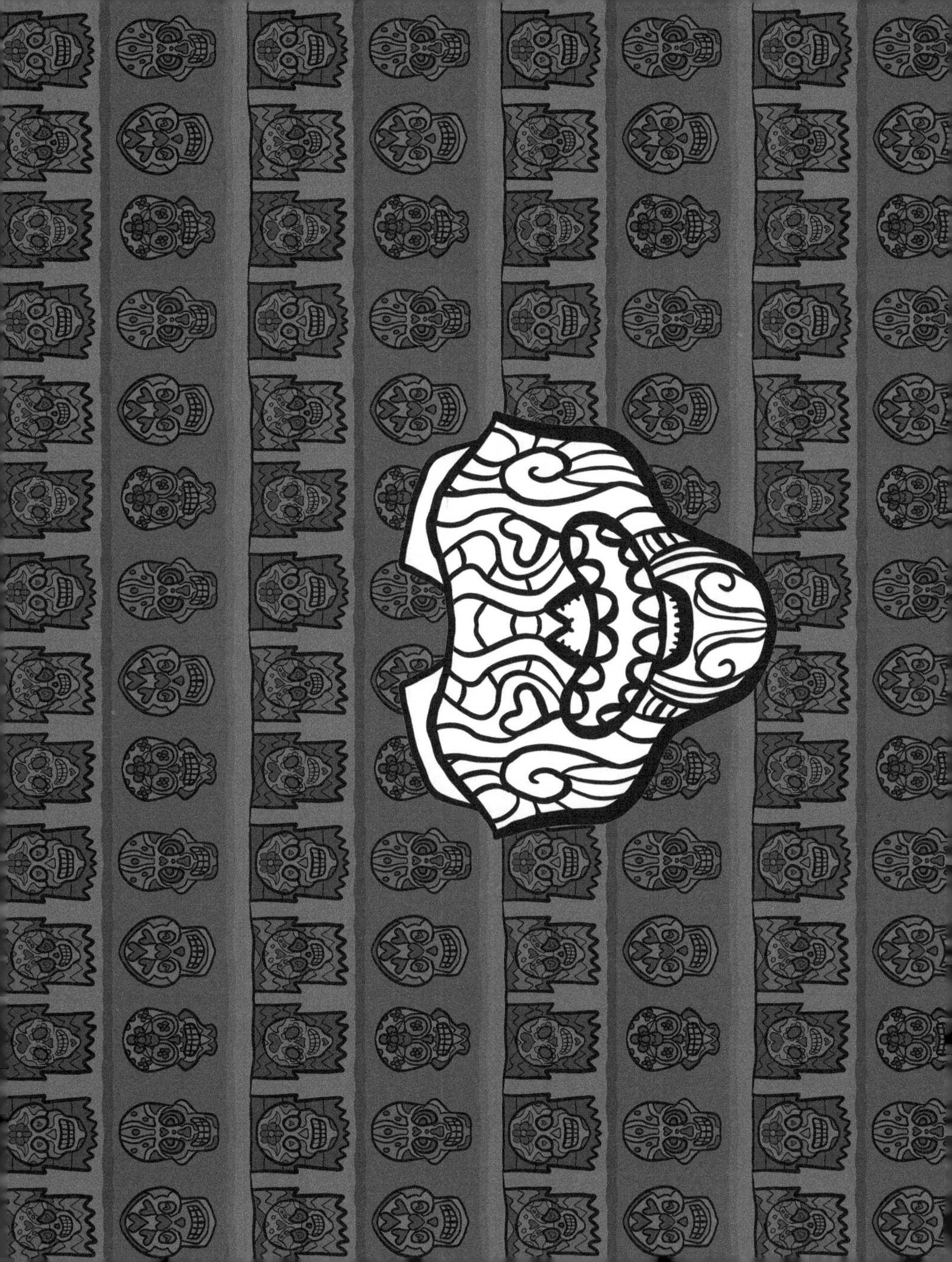

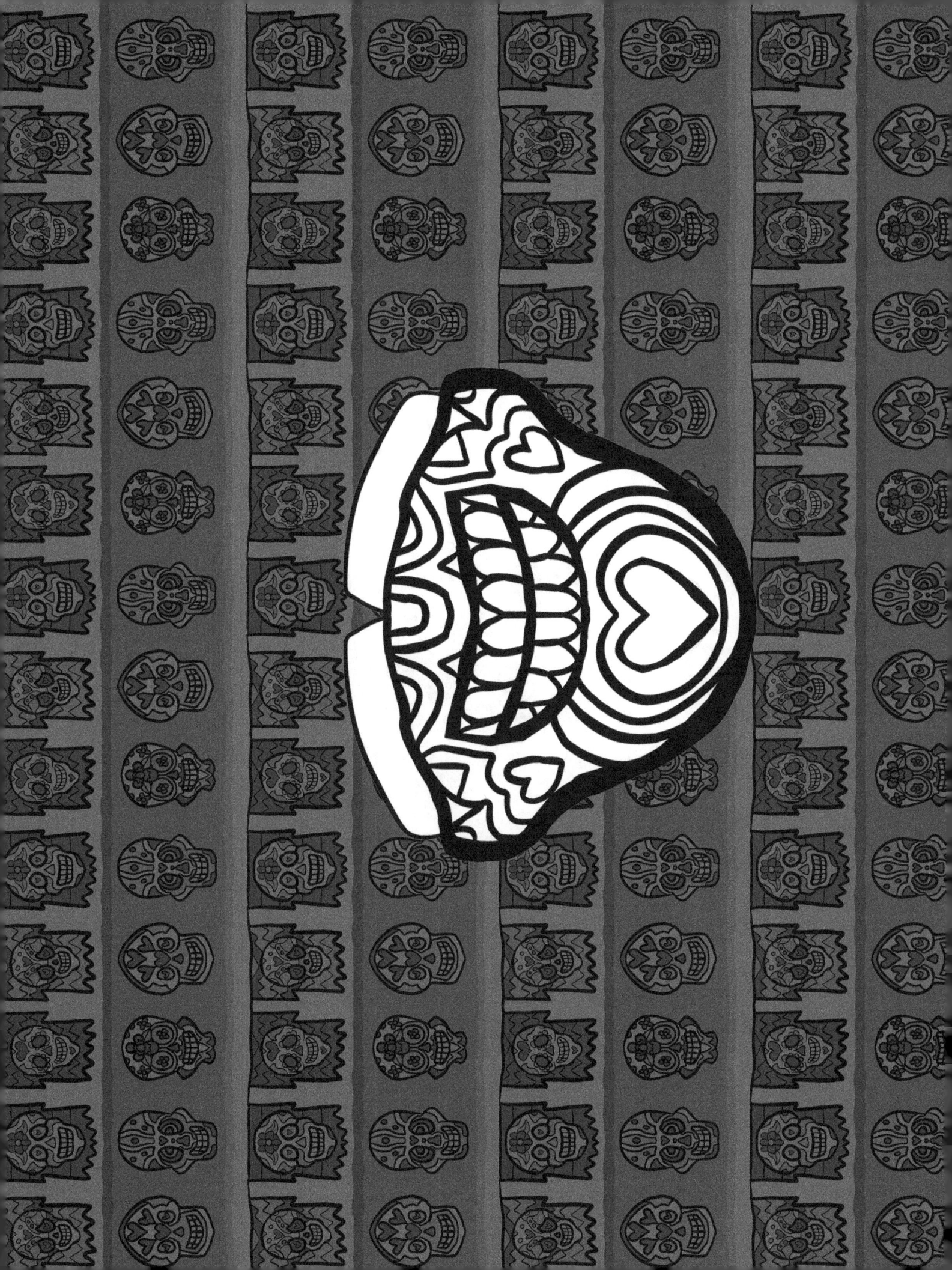

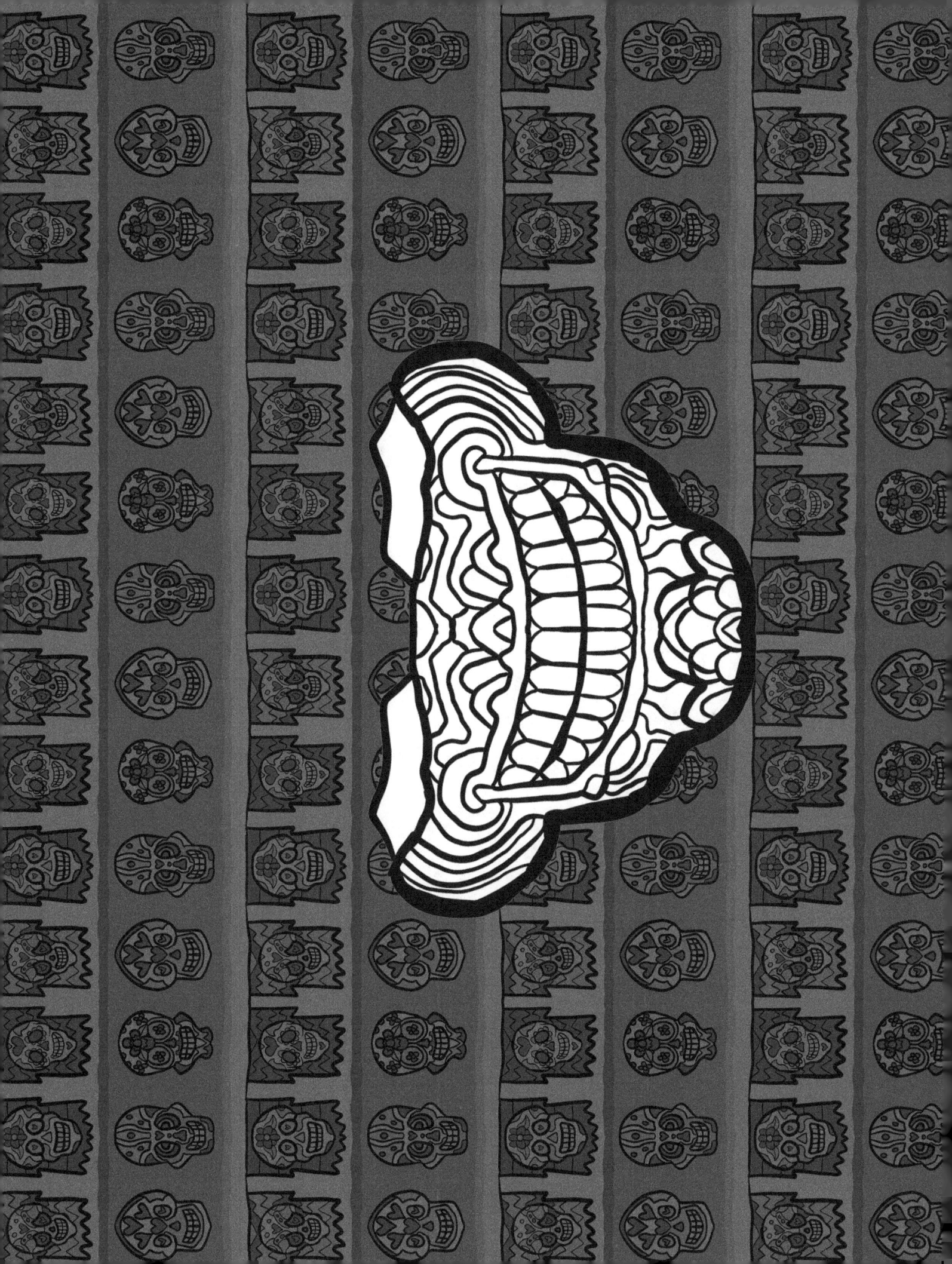

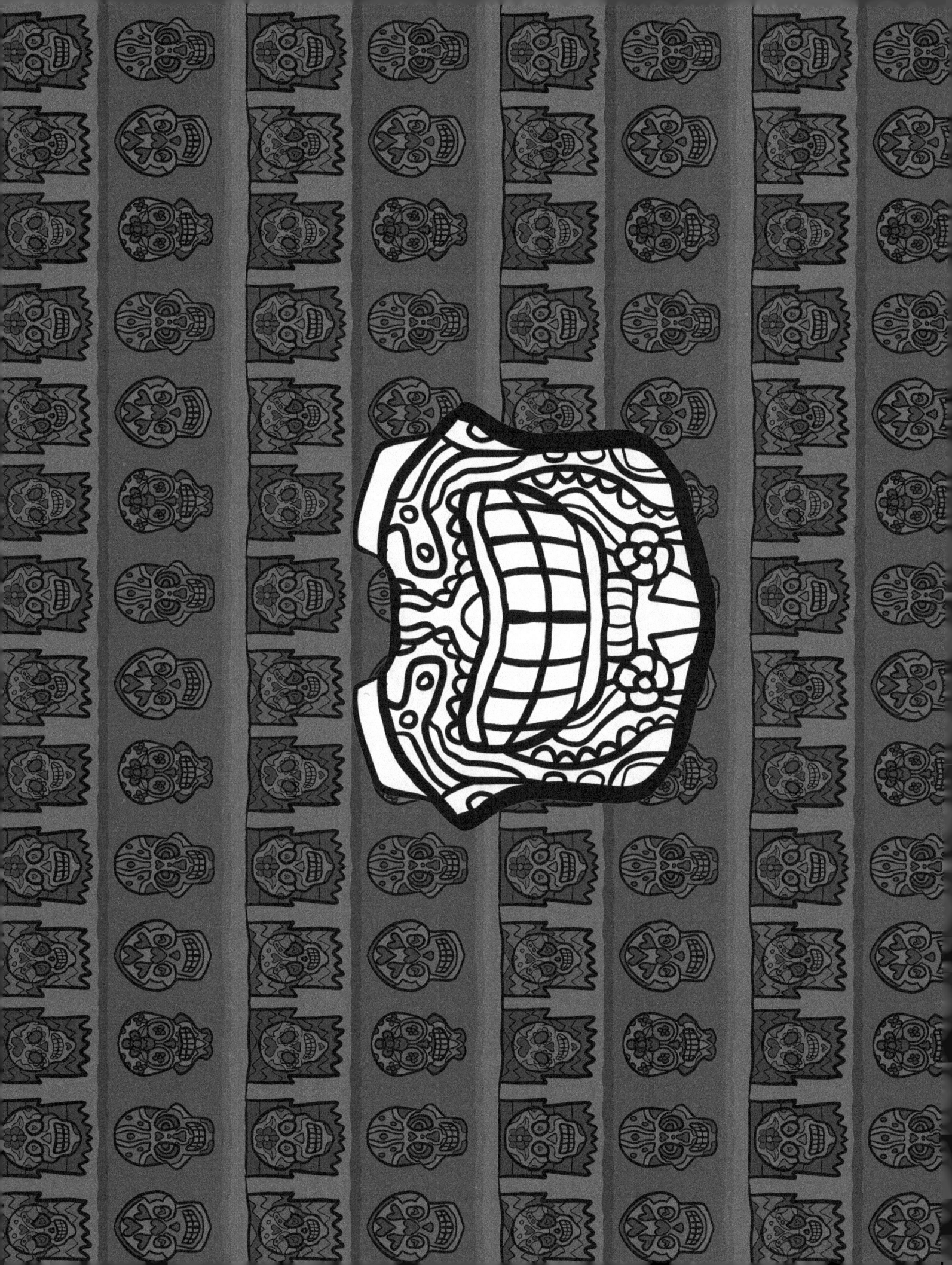

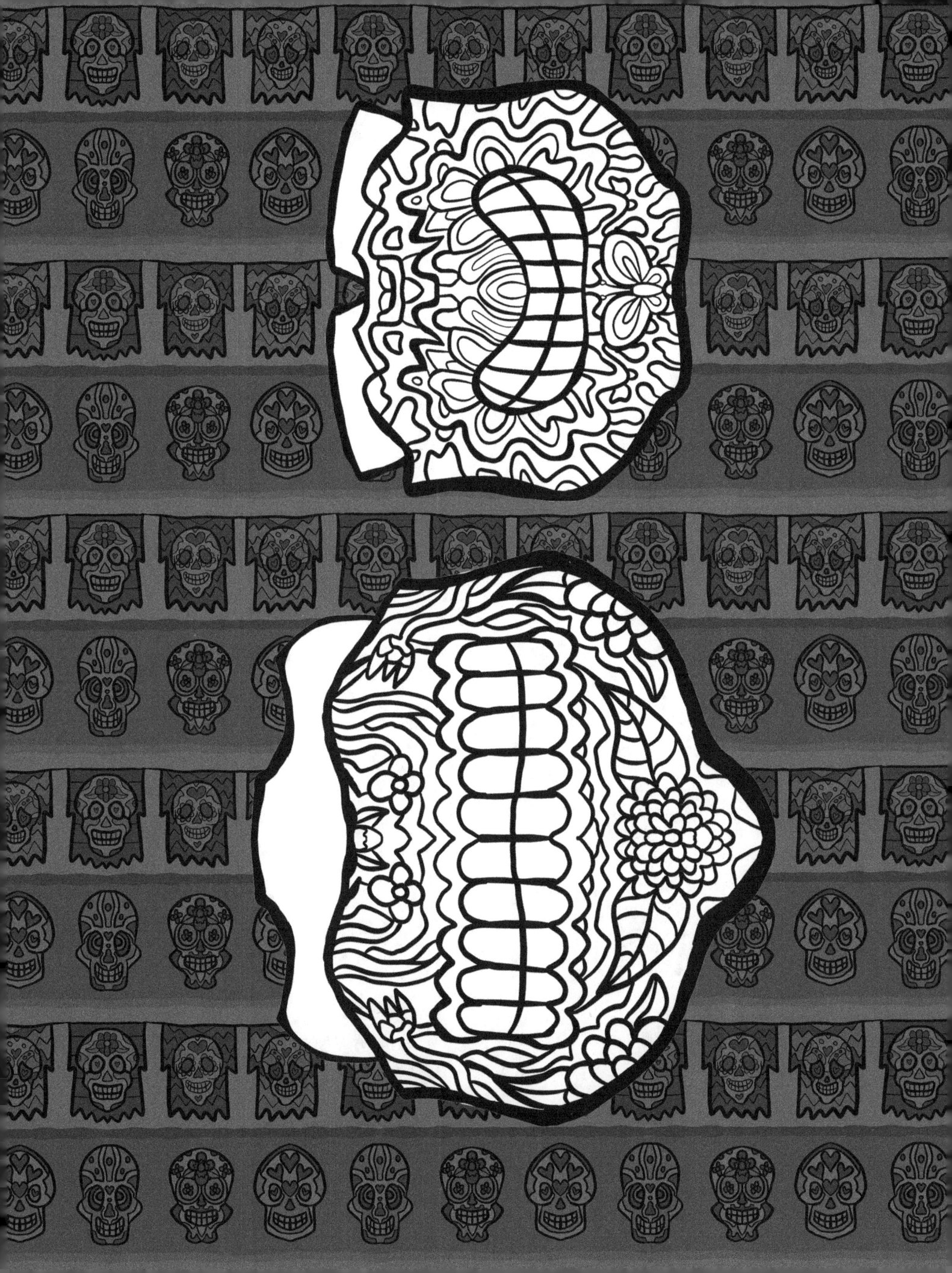

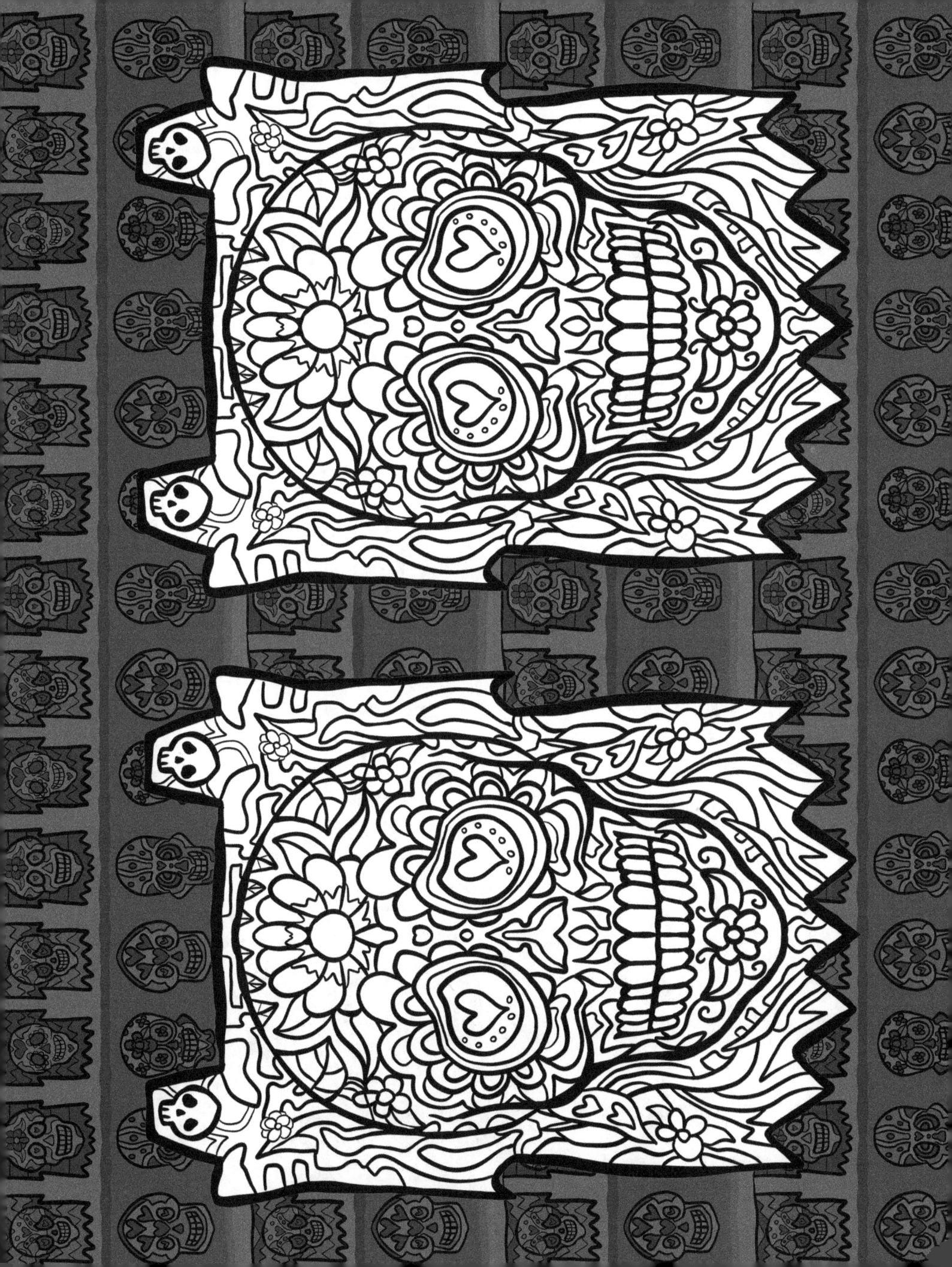

www.ingramcontent.com/pod-product-compliance
Lightning Source LLC
Chambersburg PA
CBHW081349040426
42450CB00015B/3368